G000025516

LYRICS
FROM THE CHINESE

LYRICS
FROM THE CHINESE

HELEN WADDELL

THE MALVERN PUBLISHING COMPANY LTD
1987

ISBN No: 0-947993-41-X

Published by
THE MALVERN PUBISHING COMPANY LTD

Formerly printed by T. and A. CONSTABLE Ltd
at the University Press, Edinburgh

This edition typeset by PRINTIT-NOW,
Upton-on-Severn, England
Set in Palatino

Printed in Great Britain by Ashford Colour Press
Gosport, Hampshire.

PREFACE
Dame Felicitas Corrigan

author of the Biography
'Helen Waddell'
Victor Gollanz 1986

ACKNOWLEDGEMENTS

We wish to thank Vesper
Hunter, Dame Felicitas Corrigan,
Dame Hildelith Cummings, and
Mrs Mary Martin for their
enthusiasm, dedication and
co-operation.

The Malvern Publishing
Company Ltd

PREFACE

A S the Mourne mountains on the coast of County Down sweep down to the sea, they appear at times to be sliced in two, so sheer is the drop from top to bottom. To stand on the projecting ledge of a peak and look down into the swirling waters of the chasm beneath might well induce a 'swimmingness in the eyes.' That is exactly how Helen Waddell felt in 1912 as she sat in the library of Queen's University, Belfast, idly leafing through a long-familiar book, when her eyes lighted on a few lines that suddenly captured the moment, blotted out past and future into an eternal Now, raised her to the vision spendid and changed the course of her life. A letter to her sister Meg tells the sequel:

> Do you remember the old shelf of 'Chinese Classics' by James Legge D.D., Trubner & Co., London and Hong Kong... Well, it happened on Tuesday. I had sickened my very soul over Jean de Meung and yearned for anything, by way of dry disinfectant. And I reached out to the familiar shelf, and something guided my hand to one of the

volumes I had never opened before. It opened itself at

'The gourd has still its bitter leaves'

the first of the lyrics that I send you, and I found that I was reading the prose translation of odes that were "sung at the court of Loo in the 29th year of the Duke Seang" – in the sixth century before Christ, when Confucius was eight years old.
'My breath came thick, my head swam round – for I know buried treasure when I see it, and not even the Reverend James Legge's awful and literal prose could hide the freshness of it. And in ten minutes I had written this. I'm going to give you the prose first. By the way, it's the cry of a woman who has turned her back on marriage for the sake of love.

> The gourd has still its bitter leaves
> And the crossing at the ford is deep.
> If deep, I will go through with my clothes on,
> If shallow, I will do so holding them up.
>
> The ford is full to overflowing,
> There is the note of the female pheasant.
> The full ford will not wet the axle of my carriage.
> It is the pheasant calling for her mate.

LYRICS FROM THE CHINESE

The boatman keeps beckoning
And others cross with him, but I do not,
Others cross with him, but I do not.
I am waiting for my friend.

All that the Reverend James Legge's venerably dull
word-for-word translation has succeeded in doing is to
strangle life at its source. The reader has only to turn to
Helen Waddell's rendering to realize the divine afflatus
of the true poet:

> *The gourd has still its bitter leaves,*
> *And deep the crossing at the ford.*
> *I wait my lord.*

> *The ford is brimming to its banks;*
> *The pheasant cries upon her mate.*
> *My lord is late.*

> *The boatman still keeps beckoning,*
> *And others reach their journey's end.*
> *I wait my friend.*

The poem took ten minutes to write with not a word to

alter. Within twelve hours, she had recast seven more commonplace prose passages into lyrical poems of childlike directness, within a week had added another twenty, in a short time increased the number to thirty-six, prefaced the collection with an introduction which was nothing if not brilliant, submitted her work to the eminent publishing house of Constable, and before 1913 was out saw her first book issued to the public and the talk of Dublin.

When Helen Waddell chanced upon the book that presaged her destiny, she had been tracing the development of man's conception of human love, with special relationship to Woman as a dramatic asset in pre-Shakespearian drama. Enmeshed in the thought of Western poets and their attitudes over a period of no more than two or three hundred years, she was suddenly faced with poems of the first rank, whose makers had lived twelve centuries before Christ. There is a Chinese proverb: 'The peach and the plum tree do not speak, yet around them are to be seen the footprints of men.' Against their background of morning-glory, flowering rushes, blue iris, peach blossom and green willow, almost all the poems are variants of the one story which, from then until now, the world has been telling itself since the evening and morning of the sixth day, when God took a rib from Adam as he lay asleep, built the rib into a woman, and gave him a companion like unto himself.

Lyrics from the Chinese lie within and yet far beyond

the limits of Time and Space: they speak to Everyman. While the traveller in time will often recognize his own face in the mysterious waters that flow so quietly, he will always find bends in the river leading to uncharted space, sea-coasts that stretch out to infinity. In other words, he will be given the freedom of Yuen-K'en by Helen herself and, if wise, will follow her as guide through this chief city of the province of Ch'in, for its name, as she is about to inform you, is the Chinese for Babylon.

Felicitas Corrigan O.S.B.

* * * * *

* Chinese writing numbers some 50,000 characters. The ideogram on the title page, the calligraphic symbol of Love, is reproduced by kind permission of the Carmelites of Quidenham, Norfolk.

TO MY FATHER

INTRODUCTION

IT is by candlelight one enters Babylon; and all roads lead to Babylon, provided it is by candlelight one journeys. It was by candlelight that John Milton read Diodorus Siculus, and by the Third Book he had voyaged beyond the Cape of Hope and now was past Mozambic, and already felt freshly blowing on his face

'Sabean odours from the spicie shore
Of Arabie the blest.'

It was by candlelight that the sea coast of Bohemia was discovered, and the finding of it made a winter's tale. Baghdad is not a city to be seen by day; candlelight is the only illumination for all Arabian nights.

One sees most by candlelight, because one

sees little. There is a magic ring, and in it all things shine with a yellow shining, and round it wavers the eager dark. This is the magic of the lyrics of the twelfth century in France, lit candles in 'a casement ope at night,' starring the dusk in Babylon; candles flare and gutter in the meaner streets, Villon's lyrics, these; candles flame in its cathedral-darkness, Latin hymns of the Middle Ages, of Thomas of Celano and Bernard of Morlaix. For if Babylon has its Quartier Latin, it has also its Notre Dame. The Middle Ages are the Babylon of the religious heart.

Every literature has its Babylon. Or rather, like that other Babylon, not of the spirit, Babylon is one, and all nations have drunk of her wine. She, too, is the haven desired of 'everyone that saileth any whither' by reason of her costliness, her merchandise of gold and precious stones and pearls, of fine linen and purple and silk and scarlet, thyine wood and ivory, cinnamon and incense, wine and souls of men; and this Babylon too will have fallen when the sound of the flute is no more heard in her, and 'the light of a candle shall shine no more at all.' All languages are spoken in Babylon, yet with the same accent; here are gateways of the Moors in Spain, Venetian waterways, streets of Old Paris, and over all the undiscerning twilight. All men meet in Babylon who go on pilgrimages, for all roads end in Babylon, the Road of the San Grael, the Road of the Secret Rose.

It is long since the East made good its claim to Babylon in one thousand and one nights, and now among all the taverns there is none more crowded than the Inn of the Rubaiyat; yet on the farther side the city stretches dim and all but unexplored. There are even the fragments of an old wall in the heart of it, the ruins of an 'East Gate,' and beside it the shimmering darkness of a clump of willows. The scholars - for even scholars sometimes come to Babylon - have identified it as

Yuen-K'ew, some time chief city of the province of Ch'in, but this was by daylight; the theory is only tenable if Yuen-K'ew is the Chinese for Babylon.

For the Babylon beyond the broken wall is Old Babylon; its temple-lights are Songs of Sacrifice that were old when Buddha died. There are waste places with dark pools and the ghostly gleam of lotus; black reaches of a palace moat; and once a Chinese lantern flashes on a wall leprous with lichen and hideously stained. The streets are narrow, but they climb up and up, past darkened houses and 'mounds of red earth from whose sides strange trees grow out,' and suddenly break into broad daylight, and wide grassy spaces, with the swift flight of swallows overhead. Looking down, Babylon lies in a luminous mist shot through with points of fire; but on the other side there is a great stretch of quiet water, and in its depths one sees the city of all legends, the oldest Babylon of all. There was morning glory on the trellis of the palace garden of Wei, and through fathoms of clear water one sees it yet. The very sunlight is molten, and the echoes of a drinking-song come faint but very joyous. The sound has travelled far. That water is thirty centuries deep.

It is through two stout volumes of 'The Chinese Classics' that this road to Babylon runs; a pleasant edition, printed at Hong Kong, and sold there 'At the Author's.' That author was Dr Legge, some time missionary in China, late Professor of Chinese at Oxford. He was not the first to find the road. It was a Jesuit Father of the eighteenth century, one Père Lacharme, who first passed under the 'East Gate' into the city of the Shih-King, but he wrote of it in Latin, and the book was not popular. This is the easier road; every lyric has its Chinese text, black and unfamiliar and satisfying; beneath it a prose translation of unflinching accuracy, and footnotes that

unravel all things, from the habits of a
sinister plant called tribulus - Shakespeare
would have had it in his witches cauldron - to
the wickedness of the Duke Seuen in his
palace of Wei. It is the footnotes that create so
gracious a sense of security, an atmosphere in
which even the Duke Seuen loses half his
terrors: the kindly precision of a scholar
without guile.

And a generous scholar; for at the end of
'the great travail so gladly spent,' he leaves it
to the pleasure of 'anyone who is willing to
undertake the labour... to present the pieces in
a faithful metrical version.' These stones are
from his quarry; it was under the great
Sinologue's Act of Indulgence that these lyrics
were chosen. And though their fidelity might
be a matter of dispute (in seven lines only has
the original rendering been strictly kept, the
opening line of Odes I, XI, and XXXIII, the
second and third of Ode II, and the last of
Odes XXVIII and XXXVI.), the defence was

made long ago in the preface to a seventeenth-century translation from the French, in five volumes folio. 'The translator hath but turned the wrong side of the Arras towards us, for all translations, you know, are no other,' and it was only to compensate for the original colouring that a later hand 'hath inserted... false stitches of his own.'

LYRICS FROM THE CHINESE

CONTENTS

XIII   THE SWALLOWS TAKE THEIR FLIGHT

The inner history of the Palace of Wei is something of a *'chronique scandaleuse,'* and the Duke Seuen is the heir of an evil tradition. This tragedy is before his day. Most of the commentators refer it to the dismissal in disgrace of one Tae-Kwei, a hapless and gentle lady of the harem of Duke Chwang, a dismissal preluded by the murder of her only son. It happened in 718 B.C; it is a grief that is twenty-seven centuries old.

XIV   THE WILLOWS BY THE EASTERN GATE

He complains of a broken assignation.

XV   I CANNOT COME TO YOU. I AM AFRAID

XVI   THE RUSHES ON THE MARSH ARE GREEN

XVII   I SAW THE MARSH WITH RUSHES DANK AND GREEN

XVIII   I AM GOING TO GATHER THE WHEAT

The joyous rollick of the metre would seem to suggest a rustic Don Juan, but even in the eighth century B.C. the poets had learned the uses of the pastoral, and Doctor Legge assures us that hereby three notorious court intrigues are obscurely glanced at. In brief, to quote the "Little Preface", 'A Gentleman Sings of his Intimacy with various Noble Ladies.' There is evidently an unsuspected strain of the *'gaillard'* in an imperturbable nation.

LYRICS FROM THE CHINESE

T H E gourd has still its bitter leaves,

And deep the crossing at the ford.

I wait my lord.

The ford is brimming to its banks;

The pheasant cries upon her mate.

My lord is late.

The boatman still keeps beckoning,

And others reach their journey's end.

I wait my friend.

A H, let it drift, that boat of cypress wood,

There in the middle of the Ho.

He was my mate,

And until death I will go desolate.

Ah Mother! God!

How is it that ye will not understand?

Ah, let it drift, that boat of cypress wood,

There in the middle of the Ho.

He was my King.

I swear I will not do this evil thing.

Ah Mother! God!

How is it that ye will not understand?

II *Written B.C. 826*

THE dew is heavy on the grass,

At last the sun is set.

Fill up, fill up the cups of jade,

The night's before us yet!

All night the dew will heavy lie

Upon the grass and clover.

Too soon, too soon, the dew will dry,

Too soon the night be over!

Written B.C. c.1100 III

W I T H I N the massive cup of jade

The yellow liquid shines;

Our prince is sure a man of men,

And splendid are his wines.

IV *Written B.C. 1121*

THE morning glory climbs above my head,

Pale flowers of white and purple, blue and red.

I am disquieted.

Down in the withered grasses something

 stirred;

I thought it was his footfall that I heard.

Then a grasshopper chirred.

I climbed the hill just as the new moon showed,

I saw him coming on the southern road.

My heart lays down its load.

Written B.C. c.1121 V

W E load the sacrificial stands
Of wood and earthen ware,
The smell of burning southernwood
Is heavy in the air.

It was our fathers' sacrifice,
It may be they were eased.
We know no harm to come of it;
It may be God is pleased.

VI *Written B.C. c. 1114*

I W E N T out at the Eastern Gate,

I saw the girls in clouds,

Like clouds they were, and soft and bright,

But in the crowds

I thought on the maid who is my light,

Down-drooping, soft as the grey twilight;

She is my mate.

I went out by the Tower on the Wall,

I saw the girls in flower,

Like flowering rushes they swayed and bent,

But in that hour

I thought on the maid who is my saint,

In her thin white robe and her colouring faint;

She is my all.

Written B.C. 680   VII

HO W say they that the Ho is wide,

When I could ford it if I tried?

How say they Sung is far away,

When I can see it every day?

Yet must indeed the Ho be deep,

When I have never dared the leap;

And since I am content to stay,

Sung must indeed be far away.

VIII   *Written B.C. 650*

I SEE you with your bamboo rods

Go fishing up the K'e.

Fain would I rise and come to you,

And all day long I think of you,

But I am far away.

The waters of the K'e lie east,

And west the Ts'en-yuen.

But now I am a married wife,

And maid that is a wedded wife,

She comes not home again.

The waters of the K'e lie east,

The Ts'en-yuen are west.

My white teeth flash, I smile on him,

These girdle-gems were given by him,

His wife is richly drest.

There in the river leaped a fish.

The oars dip in the K'e.

O that I might come back again,

And then I might forget again,

Forget for but a day!

IX *Written B.C. c. 700*

THE wind blows from the North.

He looks and his eyes are cold.

He looks and smiles and then goes forth,

My grief grows old.

The wind blows and the dust.

Tomorrow he swears he will come.

His words are kind, but he breaks his trust,

My heart is numb.

All day the wind blew strong,

The sun was buried deep.

I have thought of him so long, so long,

I cannot sleep.

The clouds are black with night,

The thunder brings no rain.

I wake and there is no light,

I bear my pain.

X *Written B.C. 718*

YELLOW's the robe for honour,

And green is for disgrace.

I wear the green and not the gold,

And turn away my face.

I wear the green of scorning,

Who wore the gold so long.

I think upon the Sages,

Lest I should do them wrong.

It is for her he shames me.

I sit and think apart.

I wonder if the Sages knew

A woman's heart.

THE tribulus grows on the wall,

Upon the stain.

The things done in that inner room

Men cannot name.

The tribulus grows on the wall.

The stain is old.

The evil of that inner room

May not be told.

XII   *Written B.C. 700*

THE swallows take their flight

Across the ford.

My lady goes from sight;

And I must bring her on her way,

Yet leave her ere the close of day,

So wills her lord.

The swallows take their flight,

Again they come.

My lady goes from sight;

And far must I escort her to the South,

From whence no spring-time wind nor summer

drouth

Shall bring her home.

THE willows by the Eastern Gate

Are deep in sheltering leaves.

You said 'Before the night grows late,'

— There's twittering in the eaves.

The willows by the Eastern Gate

All night in shadow are.

You said 'Before the night grows late,'

— There shines the morning star.

XIV *Written B.C. 826*

I CANNOT come to you. I am afraid.

I will not come to you. There, I have said.

Though all the night I lie awake and know

That you are lying, waking, even so.

Though day by day you take the lonely road,

And come at nightfall to a dark abode.

Yet if so be you are indeed my friend,

Then in the end,

There is one road, a road I've never gone,

And down that road you shall not pass alone.

And there's one night you'll find me by your side.

The night that they shall tell me you have died.

THE rushes on the marsh are green,
And in the wind they bend.
I saw a woman walking there,
Near daylight's end.

On the black water of the marsh,
The lotus buds swim white.
I saw her standing by the verge
At fall of night.

All the long night I lie awake,

And sleep I cannot find.

I see her slim as any rush

Sway in the wind.

I shut my eyes and see again

The whiteness of her throat,

On the black water of the night

Like lotus float.

Written c. B.C. 605 XVI

I S A W the marsh with rushes dank and green,

And deep black pools beneath a sunset sky,

And lotus silver bright

Gleam on their blackness in the dying light,

As I passed by.

And all that night I saw as in a dream

Her fair face lifted up

Shine in the darkness like a lotus cup,

Snow-white against the deep black pool of night,

Till dawn was nigh.

XVII *A variant of the same*

I AM going to gather the wheat

In the fields of Mei.

But my thoughts are not on the whitening wheat.

Fairest and fair of the maids of the Keang,

She whom I met at the fair of Sang-chung,

She is to meet me in far Shang-kung,

And then for the road with me through

Ke-shang,

And into the fields of Mei.

I am going to gather the millet

In the north of Mei.

But my thoughts are not on the new-mown

millet.

Fairest and fair of the maids of the Yung,

She whom I met at the fair of Sang-chung,

She is to meet me in far Shang-kung,

And then for the road with me through

Ke-shang,

And into the north of Mei.

I am going to gather the rye,

In the east of Mei.

But my thoughts are not on the ripening rye.

Fairest and fair of the maids of the Wang,

She whom I met at the fair of Sang-chung,

She is to meet me in far Shang-kung,

And then for the road with me through

Ke-shang,

And into the east of Mei.

XVIII *Written c. B.C.700*

THE K'e still ripples to its banks,

The moorfowl cry.

My hair was gathered in a knot,

And you came by.

Selling of silk you were, a lad

Not of our kin;

You passed at sunset on the road

From far-off Ts'in.

The frogs were croaking in the dusk;

The grass was wet.

We talked together, and I laughed;

I hear it yet.

I thought that I would be your wife;

I had your word.

And so I took the road with you,

And crossed the ford.

I do not know when first it was

Your eyes looked cold.

But all this was three years ago.

And I am old.

XIX *Written B.C. 718*

MY lord is gone away to serve the King.

The pigeons homing at the set of sun

Are side by side upon the courtyard wall,

And far away I hear the herdsmen call

The goats upon the hill when day is done.

But I, I know not when he will come home.

I live the days alone.

My lord is gone away to serve the King.

I hear a pigeon stirring in the nest,

And in the field a pheasant crying late.

— She has not far to go to find her mate.

There is a hunger will not let me rest.

The days have grown to months and months to
years,

And I have no more tears.

Written B.C. 769 XX

I WOULD have gone to my lord in his need,

Have galloped there all the way,

But this is a matter concerns the State,

And I, being a woman, must stay.

I watched them leaving the palace yard,

In carriage and robe of state.

I would have gone by the hills and the fords;

I know they will come too late.

I may walk in the garden and gather

Lilies of mother-of-pearl.

I had a plan would have saved the State.

— But mine are the thoughts of a girl.

The Elder Statesmen sit on the mats,

And wrangle through half the day;

A hundred plans they have drafted and dropped,

And mine was the only way.

THE wise man's wisdom is our strength,

The woman's wisdom is our bane.

The men build up the city walls

For women to tear down again.

No man from any woman's wit

Hath yet learned aught of any worth,

For wise is she, but unto ill,

To bring disorder on the earth.

What does she in affairs of State?

Her place is in the inner room.

Her wisdom doth least hurt in this,

To mind the silkworm and the loom.

XXII *Written B.C. 780*

WHEN first the guests approach the mats

Their manners are correct;

And even when they well have drunk,

They still are circumspect.

But when the guests have drunk too much,

They lose sobriety;

They shout and brawl and loudly sing,

— An impropriety.

If when a guest has drunk too much

He courteously depart,

His host and he would happy be,

Each having done his part.

But to remain when one is drunk

Is not a virtuous thing.

To drinking, though a custom good,

One must deportment bring.

XXIII *Written B.C. 780*

No man is in the fields,

The forest's stripped and bare,

A few poor faggots left,

And there is none to care.

These men are in great place,

And still they grind the State.

The people cry to heaven,

And think that God is great.

— Is He too great to hate?

I SEE on high the Milky Way,

But here's a rougher road.

The Sacred Oxen shining stand;

They do not draw our load.

The Sieve is sparkling in the South,

But good and ill come through.

The Ladle opens wide its mouth,

And pours out naught for you.

At dawn the Weaving Sisters sleep,

At dusk they rise again;

But though their Shining Shuttle flies,

They weave no robe for men.

XXV *Written B.C. 780*

IF there are fish within the trap,
They'll churn it as they leap.
If none, you'll see the water black,
And stars in it asleep.

— The water in the trap is black,
The stars are shining still —
If some men get enough to eat,
There's few can get their fill.

Written B.C. 780 XXVI

UNDER the pondweed do the great fish go,

In the green darkness where the rushes grow.

The King is in Hao.

Under the pondweed do the great fish lie:

Down in Hao the sunny hours go by.

The King holds revelry.

Under the pondweed do the great fish sleep;

The dragon-flies are drowsy in the heat.

The King is drinking deep.

XXVII *Written B.C. 780*

B E F O R E the snow comes sleet,

And wind from out the East.

One moment may let slip

Our goodly fellowship.

Death clutches at our feet.

Who knows when next we meet?

Yet still the wine is sweet.

O King, enjoy the feast!

PEACH blossom after rain

　Is deeper red;

　The willow fresher green;

　Twittering overhead;

　And fallen petals lie wind-blown,

　Unswept upon the courtyard stone.

XXIX *Written under the T'ang dynasty*

THE world is weary, hasting on its road,

Is it worth while to add its cares to thine?

Seek for some grassy place to pour the wine,

And find an idle hour to sing an ode.

YOU'VE two score, three score years before
 you yet,

And at the end of them your day is done.

A thousand plans you have before you set:

Is it worth while to weary over one?

Now, when the gods have made an idle day,

Take it, and let the idle hours go by;

And when the gods three cups before you lay,

Lift them, and drain them dry.

XXXI *From Sir John Davies' 'Poetry of the Chinese.'*

BLUE iris sweetest smells,

Upon its stem unbroken.

A woman highest sells,

With her fair name unspoken.

From Sir John Davies' 'Poetry of the Chinese.' XXXII

O N the moor is the creeping grass,

Parched, thirsting for the dew,

And over it the swallows dip and pass,

The live-long summer through.

I came at sunset, fevered with the heat,

On the moor is the creeping grass,

Deep-drenchèd with the dew,

And over it the swallows dip and pass,

The live-long summer through.

You came at sunrise, ere the dew was dried.

And I am satisfied.

XXXIII   *Written in the seventh century before Christ.*

THE moon is shining on this borderland,

Just as it will be shining on Lung-t'ow.

The sea is very quiet on the sand;

I wonder what the folk are doing now.

The wild geese settle with the same old cry,

The moonlight sleeps upon the threshold stone.

The millet in the field is shoulder high,

And my young wife goes up the path alone.

Written under the T'ang dynasty XXXIV

HOW goes the night?

Midnight has still to come.

Down in the court the torch is blazing bright;

I hear far off the throbbing of the drum.

How goes the night?

The night is not yet gone.

I hear the trumpets blowing on the height;

The torch is paling in the coming dawn.

How goes the night?

The night is past and done.

The torch is smoking in the morning light,

The dragon banner floating in the sun.

XXXV *Written in the ninth century before Christ.*

WHITE clouds are in the sky.

Great shoulders of the hills

Between us two must lie.

The road is rough and far.

Deep fords between us are.

I pray you not to die.

Written B.C. 1121 XXXVI

ENVOI

-

Immortal in thy passion and thy pain,

For ever crowned art thou,

The dew of the eternal cap on thy head,

Its light upon thy brow.

On a copy of the first edition of LYRICS FROM
THE CHINESE, there is an amendment in Helen
Waddell's own handwriting.   She has scored
through poem XV and written beneath it —

I CANNOT come to you. I am afraid.

I will not come to you. There, I have said.

Though all the night I lie awake and know

That you are lying, waking, even so.

Though day by day you take the lonely road,

And come at nightfall to a dark abode.

Yet if so be you are indeed my friend,

Then in the end,

There is one road, a road I've never gone,

And down that road you shall not pass alone.

And there's one night you'll find me by your side.

The night that they shall tell me you have died.

Living we lie asunder.

Dead we shall share one grave.

ISBN 0-947993-41-X

00795